Welcome to my lunch recipes book, where you'll find a variety of delicious and easy-to-follow recipes to make your midday meals more exciting and satisfying. Whether you're looking for quick and healthy options for busy weekdays or indulgent treats for lazy weekends, this book has something for everyone. From classic sandwiches and salads to exotic dishes from around the world, these recipes are sure to add some flavor to your lunch routine. So, grab your apron and get ready to explore the world of delicious lunch recipes!

Baked Potato Bar

Ingredients

5 pounds baked potatoes.
3-5 pounds pulled pork cooked.
2 cups sharp cheddar cheese shredded.
1/2 pound bacon cooked & crumbled.
1 cup sour cream.
1/2 cup chives chopped.
2 cups broccoli cooked.
1 bottle bbq sauce.

A baked potato bar is an easy and healthy dinner option for kids, and it's simple to prepare. Start by baking five pounds of potatoes according to the instructions on the package. While they're cooking, pre-cook three to five pounds of pulled pork as well as one-half pound of bacon. Once the potatoes are done, split them open and sprinkle two cups of shredded sharp cheddar cheese over the top. Then, add the cooked pulled pork, crumbled bacon, one cup of sour cream, half a cup of chopped chives and two cups of cooked broccoli. Finally, make sure to provide some BBQ sauce for everyone to enjoy. With minimal effort, you can create a delicious and nutritious baked potato bar that all the kids will love! Enjoy!

Arugula Pizza

INGREDIENTS

1 ¼ cup pizza sauce (purchased or our favorite Easy Pizza Sauce)
1 cup (3 ounces) shredded smoked gouda cheese.
½ cup shredded Parmesan cheese.
6 ounces fresh mozzarella cheese.
4 cups (3 ounces) baby arugula.
1 tablespoon extra virgin olive oil.
¼ teaspoon kosher salt, plus more for sprinkling.

If you're looking for delicious pizza recipes, look no further than this delicious arugula pizza. This delicious and easy-to-prepare meal is perfect for any day of the week. To make it, start by preheating your oven to 500°F (260°C). Next, spread 1 ¼ cups of purchased or homemade pizza sauce on a 12 inch baking sheet lined with parchment paper. Top with 1 cup (3 ounces) shredded smoked gouda cheese, ½ cup shredded Parmesan cheese, and 6 ounces fresh mozzarella cheese. Bake in the preheated oven for 10 minutes until golden brown and bubbly. Once done baking, top the pizza with 4 cups (3 ounces) baby arugula and sprinkle with 1 tablespoon extra virgin olive oil and ¼ teaspoon kosher salt. Slice, serve, and enjoy! With its delicious combination of flavors, this delicious arugula pizza is sure to become a family favorite. Enjoy!

Baked Feta Pasta

ingredients

2 pints (20 oz) grape tomatoes.
1/2 cup extra-virgin olive oil.
Salt and freshly ground black pepper.
7 oz. block feta cheese (sheep's milk variety), drained.
10 oz. dry pasta (bite size)
5 medium garlic cloves, peeled and halved.
8 oz. ...
1/4 tsp crushed red pepper flakes, or more to taste.

Baked Feta Pasta is an easy and healthy dish that takes only minimal time to prepare. With just a handful of simple ingredients, you can create this delicious meal. To make it, start by preheating your oven to 425 degrees Fahrenheit.

In a large bowl, combine the grape tomatoes, extra-virgin olive oil, salt and pepper. Cut the feta cheese into small cubes and add it to the bowl. Next, cook 10 oz of bite-size pasta according to package instructions until al dente. Once done, drain it and mix it with the tomato mixture in the bowl.

Add garlic cloves, 8 oz of mushrooms (sliced), and 1/4 tsp of crushed red pepper flakes, or to taste. Toss everything together and spread it in a single layer on an oven-safe dish. Bake for 25 minutes until the top is lightly golden brown.

Baked Feta Pasta is now ready to enjoy! Serve with a sprinkling of fresh herbs, extra olive oil, and a side of crusty bread. This healthy pasta dish makes for a great weeknight dinner that is sure to please the whole family.
Enjoy!

Chicken Fajitas

Here is a list of ingredients for chicken fajitas:
- 1 pound boneless, skinless chicken breasts or thighs, sliced into thin strips
- 2 bell peppers (any color), sliced
- 1 large onion, sliced
- 3 tablespoons lime juice
- 2 tablespoons olive oil
- 2 teaspoons chili powder
- 1 teaspoon paprika
- 1 teaspoon cumin
- 1 teaspoon garlic powder
- Salt and pepper, to taste
- 8-10 flour or corn tortillas
- Optional toppings: shredded cheese, sour cream, avocado, salsa, fresh cilantro, etc.

Instructions:
1. In a large bowl, mix together the lime juice, olive oil, chili powder, paprika, cumin, garlic powder, salt, and pepper.
2. Add the chicken, bell peppers, and onions to the bowl and toss to coat with the marinade. Let marinate for at least 30 minutes, or up to 2 hours.
3. Heat a large skillet or griddle over high heat. Add the marinated chicken and vegetables to the skillet, and cook for 5-7 minutes, until the chicken is cooked through and the vegetables are tender.
4. Warm the tortillas in the microwave or on a griddle.
5. To assemble the fajitas, place a few spoonfuls of the chicken and vegetables mixture onto a tortilla, and top with your favorite toppings. Roll up the tortilla and enjoy!

Pulled Chicken Salad

1 small roasted chicken, about 1kg
½ red cabbage, cored and finely sliced
3 carrots, coarsely grated or finely shredded
5 spring onions, finely sliced on the diagonal
2 red chillies, halved and thinly sliced
A small bunch of coriander, roughly chopped, including stalks

Instructions for preparing Pulled Chicken Salad:

Remove the meat from the roasted chicken and shred it into bite-sized pieces using two forks or your hands.

In a large bowl, mix together the shredded chicken, finely sliced red cabbage, grated carrots, finely sliced spring onions, thinly sliced red chillies, and chopped coriander.

Season the salad with salt and pepper, to taste.

To serve, arrange the salad on a large platter or divide it evenly onto individual plates. You can also drizzle some vinaigrette or your favorite dressing over the salad, if desired.

Serve the Pulled Chicken Salad immediately and enjoy!

Mac And Cheese

Ingredients

8 ounces uncooked elbow macaroni.
¼ cup salted butter.
3 tablespoons all-purpose flour. Great Value All-Purpose Flour, 5LB. ...
2 ½ cups milk, or more as needed.
2 cups shredded sharp Cheddar cheese.
½ cup finely grated Parmesan cheese. ...
salt and ground black pepper to taste (Optional)

Making macaroni and cheese is a healthy and easy dinner for kids, as it is an excellent source of calcium and protein. With the right ingredients, you can make this classic dish in minutes.

To get started, bring a large pot of salted water to a boil over high heat. Add 8 ounces of uncooked elbow macaroni, and cook until al dente (about 7 minutes). Drain the cooked pasta in a colander.

Meanwhile, melt ¼ cup of salted butter in a large saucepan over medium heat. Add 3 tablespoons of all-purpose flour to the melted butter, stirring constantly until the mixture thickens slightly and becomes a paste. Slowly add 2 ½ cups of milk to the saucepan, continually stirring until fully incorporated and thickened.

Remove the pan from heat and stir in 2 cups of shredded sharp Cheddar cheese, ½ cup of finely grated Parmesan cheese, and salt and ground black pepper to taste (optional). Add the cooked macaroni to the saucepan and mix until all of the pasta is evenly coated.

Serve the macaroni and cheese hot, with extra Parmesan cheese sprinkled on top if desired. Enjoy!

Meatball Spaghetti

Ingredients
3 slices white bread, (crusts removed), diced or torn to pieces.
2/3 cup cold water.
1 lb lean ground beef, (7%-15% fat)
1 lb Sweet Ground Italian sausage, casings removed.
1/4 cup grated parmesan cheese, plus more to serve.
4 cloves garlic, minced.
1 tsp sea salt.
1/2 tsp black pepper.

Meatball spaghetti is a delicious, healthy and easy dinner for kids that can be prepared in no time. To make this dish start by preheating the oven to 350°F. Then, in a medium bowl, combine the diced bread and water and let it sit for 3 minutes before adding the ground beef, sausage, parmesan cheese, garlic, salt and pepper. Mix together until all ingredients are evenly distributed. After that, form 1 ½ inch balls of the meatball mixture and place them on a lightly greased baking sheet. Bake for 20-25 minutes or until the internal temperature reaches 165°F. Once done, serve over spaghetti with extra parmesan cheese if desired. Enjoy!

Chicken Tortellini

Ingredients

2 tablespoons olive oil.
8 oz boneless skinless chicken breast, cut into 1/4-inch slices.
3 cups fresh small broccoli florets.
2 teaspoons chopped garlic.
1 1/2 cups Progresso™ chicken broth (from 32-oz carton)
2 packages (9 oz each) refrigerated cheese tortellini.
1 cup milk.

Preparing a healthy and easy dinner for the kids doesn't have to be a hassle. This delicious Chicken Tortellini is sure to please everyone at the table.

To make this dish, start by heating two tablespoons of olive oil in a large skillet over medium-high heat. Once it's hot, add the chicken slices and cook for about 4 minutes until they're no longer pink. Add the broccoli florets, garlic, and a pinch of salt, then cook for another 3 to 4 minutes.

Next, pour in the Progresso™ chicken broth and bring it to a boil over high heat. Once boiling, add the tortellini and cook for about 8 minutes until the pasta is cooked through. Then, reduce the heat to low and stir in the milk. Simmer for a few more minutes until it thickens up a bit. Taste and season with salt and pepper if needed.

Serve the tortellini with some extra grated Parmesan cheese on top. Enjoy! This Chicken Tortellini is a healthy and delicious dinner that your kids are sure to love. It's quick and easy, ready in just 30 minutes. Enjoy!

*Note: You can customize this dish with other vegetables like mushrooms, bell peppers or spinach. For added protein, you can also add shrimp or cooked sausage. Enjoy!

Enjoy! With its delicious flavor and simple preparation, this Chicken Tortellini is a surefire winner for any family dinner. It's the perfect healthy and easy dinner for kids - ready in just 30 minutes! Bon appetit!

Creamy Tomato Soup

Tomato Soup is a great lunch choice for kids because it's easy to make and packed with healthy ingredients. Plus, they will love the bright and vibrant colour! Here's what you'll need to make this delicious tomato soup recipe:

- 1-1.25kg/2lb 4oz-2lb 12oz ripe tomatoes

- 1 medium onion

- 1 small carrot

- 1 celery stick

- 2 tbsp olive oil

- 2 squirts of tomato purée (about 2 tsp)

- A good pinch of sugar

- 2 bay leaves

Once you've gathered all the ingredients, it's time to start cooking! Begin by heating the olive oil in a large saucepan and adding the diced onion, carrot, celery stick. Cook over medium heat for about 5 minutes until softened. Then add the tomatoes, purée, bay leaves and sugar. Cover with a lid and cook for 40 minutes. Once the soup is cooked, remove the bay leaves and blend until smooth with a blender.

Serve up this delicious tomato soup with some crusty bread or croutons on top and you have an easy, healthy lunch that your kids will love! Enjoy!

Spinach And Feta Pizza

Ingredients

2 large Pizza Bases (see notes)
½ cup Tomato Paste.
½ Brown / Yellow Onion, finely diced.
½ Red Capsicum / Bell Pepper, finely diced.
100g / 3.5 oz Baby Spinach, roughly chopped.
4 White Mushrooms, thinly sliced.
½ cup Feta Cheese, crumbled.
1 ½ cups Shredded Mozzarella Cheese (or more, to taste)

Making delicious spinach and feta pizzas is easy and delicious. To begin, preheat your oven to 200°C / 392°F. Place the pizza bases on a lightly greased baking tray. Spread a thin layer of tomato paste over each base, then scatter the diced onion, capsicum / bell pepper, mushrooms, baby spinach and crumbled feta cheese over the top. Sprinkle with mozzarella cheese (you can add more if desired). Bake for 15-20 minutes or until golden brown and bubbly. Serve hot! Enjoy your delicious spinach and feta pizza!

These delicious spinach and feta pizzas are sure to become a family favorite in no time! The combination of flavors from the vegetables, feta and mozzarella cheese makes for a delicious meal that is sure to please everyone. With just a few simple ingredients, you can easily make delicious pizza recipes at home with ease! No need to order take-out anymore - now you can make delicious pizzas right in your own kitchen. Enjoy!

Baked Fish

Here's a list of ingredients for a baked fish recipe:

White fish fillets
Cherry tomatoes
Red onion
Garlic
Green olives
Capers
Fresh parsley
Olive oil
Dried oregano
Lemon juice
Salt and pepper, to taste

Instructions:

Preheat the oven to 375°F (190°C).

Line a baking dish with parchment paper or lightly grease it with oil.

Rinse the fish fillets and pat them dry with paper towels. Place them in the prepared baking dish.

Slice the cherry tomatoes in half and arrange them around the fish fillets.

Thinly slice the red onion and scatter it over the tomatoes.

Mince the garlic and sprinkle it over the onions.

Add the green olives and capers to the dish.

Chop the fresh parsley and sprinkle it over the top of the fish.

Drizzle the dish with olive oil and sprinkle with dried oregano.

Squeeze the lemon juice over the dish and season with salt and pepper, to taste.

Bake the fish in the preheated oven for 20-25 minutes, or until the fish is opaque and flakes easily with a fork.

Serve the baked fish hot, garnished with additional chopped parsley, if desired. Enjoy!

Shrimp Pasta

Ingredients

8 ounces fettuccine.
1 pound medium shrimp, peeled and deveined.
Kosher salt and freshly ground black pepper, to taste.
8 tablespoons 1 stick unsalted butter, divided.
4 cloves garlic, minced.
½ teaspoon dried oregano.
½ teaspoon crushed red pepper flakes.
2 cups baby arugula.

Shrimp Pasta is a healthy and easy dinner for kids that you can whip up in no time. To prepare it, start by bringing a large pot of salted water to a boil over high heat. Once boiling, add the fettuccine and cook until al dente according to package directions. Drain pasta into a colander and set aside.

Meanwhile, in a large skillet over medium heat, melt 4 tablespoons of butter. Add the shrimp and season with salt and pepper to taste. Cook, stirring occasionally until pink and cooked through, about 3-4 minutes; set aside.

To the same skillet add remaining butter, garlic, oregano and red pepper flakes. Cook, stirring frequently, until fragrant, about 1-2 minutes. Stir in the cooked pasta and shrimp; season with salt and pepper to taste.

Finally, stir in the arugula until wilted, about 1 minute. Serve immediately, garnished with more red pepper flakes if desired. Enjoy!

Chicken Quesadillas

Ingredients

1 pound skinless, boneless chicken breast, diced.
1 (1.27 ounce) packet fajita seasoning.
1 tablespoon vegetable oil.
2 green bell peppers, chopped.
2 red bell peppers, chopped.
1 onion, chopped. ...
10 (10 inch) flour tortillas.
1 (8 ounce) package shredded Cheddar cheese.

Chicken quesadillas make for a healthy and easy dinner for the whole family. To start preparing, dice the boneless chicken breasts and season with fajita seasoning. In a large skillet over medium heat, heat vegetable oil and add in the diced chicken breast, green bell peppers, red bell peppers, and onions. Cook until vegetables are softened and chicken is cooked through. To assemble the quesadillas, place about ¼ cup of cheese onto one side of a tortilla. Top with cooked vegetables and chicken, then add another ¼ cup of cheese to the top. Fold over into a half-moon shape and cook in a skillet on medium-high heat until golden brown. Repeat this process with the remaining tortillas. Serve warm and enjoy!

For a fun variation, try adding black beans to the quesadillas or swapping out Cheddar cheese for Monterey Jack. Using flavorful ingredients like jalapenos, salsa, and guacamole can also liven up this classic dish. Chicken quesadillas make for a healthy and delicious dinner that can be customized to fit the tastes of any family. Enjoy!

Chicken And Bacon Pasta

Ingredients needed
- boneless skinless chicken breast.
- smoked pancetta lardons (or bacon)
- chicken stock (made from a stock cube)
- parsley.
- garlic.
- onion.
- double cream.
- pasta shells.

Are you looking for delicious recipes that the whole family can enjoy? Look no further than this delicious chicken and bacon pasta! This delicious dish is perfect for picky eaters, and it's easy to make too. To get started, you'll need boneless skinless chicken breast, smoked pancetta lardons (or bacon), chicken stock (made from a stock cube), parsley, garlic, onion, double cream and some pasta shells.

Once you have all the ingredients ready to go, it's time to start cooking! Begin by heating up some butter or oil in a large saucepan over medium heat. Once the butter is melted, add the lardons and cook until golden. Add the garlic and onion to the pan, cooking for about 2 minutes until fragrant. Then add in the chicken breast and cook for 4-5 minutes, stirring occasionally.

Next, add the chicken stock to the pan and bring it to a gentle simmer before adding in the cream and parsley. Stir everything together and reduce the heat to low. Let the sauce simmer for about 10-15 minutes until it has reduced and thickened.

Finally, add in your cooked pasta shells and stir them through the sauce. Serve hot with a sprinkle of parsley on top and enjoy! With this delicious chicken and bacon pasta recipe, you'll have a meal that kids and adults will love. Enjoy!

Tuna Pasta

Ingredients

2 tablespoons olive oil.
2 large cloves garlic minced.
1 (5 ounce) can tuna, drained I prefer tuna packed in oil.
1 teaspoon lemon juice.
1 tablespoon fresh parsley chopped.
Salt & pepper to taste.
4 ounces uncooked pasta (I used spaghetti)

Tuna pasta is a delicious and easy-to-make recipe for kids. It's perfect for busy weeknights when you don't have much time to cook. To make this delicious dish, start by heating the olive oil in a large skillet over medium heat. Add the garlic and sauté until fragrant, about 1 minute. Add the tuna and stir to combine. Then add the lemon juice and parsley, season with salt and pepper to taste, and cook for another minute or two. Finally, add the uncooked pasta to the skillet and mix everything together. Cook according to directions on the box until al dente. Serve hot and enjoy! Tuna pasta is a delicious and nutritious meal that your kids will love. Enjoy!

Grilled Hot Dogs

Grilled hot dogs are a classic summer cookout favorite. They're also an easy and healthy dinner option for kids. Preparing grilled hot dogs is super simple - all you need to do is gather the ingredients, heat up your grill, and get cooking!

To prepare grilled hot dogs, you'll need eight hot dogs, ¼ cup ketchup, 2 Tbsp Worcestershire Sauce, 1 minced garlic clove, and 1 tsp of vegetable oil. Start by preheating the grill to medium-high heat. Once it's hot enough, place the hot dogs on the grill and cook for about 8 minutes or until browned and cooked through.

In a small bowl, mix together the ketchup, Worcestershire sauce, garlic and vegetable oil. Brush the hot dogs with the mixture when they come off of the grill. Serve with your favorite condiments and sides for a delicious summer meal! Enjoy!

Salmon And Cream Cheese Sandwich

Ingredients
Bread. ...
Whipped Cream Cheese. ...
Smoked Salmon. ...
Fresh Chives. ...
Fresh Parsley. ...
Salt and Black Pepper.

This easy-to-make sandwich is a great way to introduce kids to the delicious flavors of smoked salmon! Start by taking two slices of whole wheat bread and spreading a generous layer of whipped cream cheese on one side. Layer on some thinly sliced smoked salmon, and top with fresh chives, parsley, salt and black pepper for flavor. Serve up with a side of fruit for a healthy, delicious and fun lunch that the kids will love! Enjoy!

Easy Chicken Salad

INGREDIENTS
3 CUPS COOKED CHICKEN, DICED,
(I LIKE TO USE ROTISSERIE CHICKEN)
1/2 CUP MAYONNAISE.
1/2 CUP FINELY CHOPPED
CELERY.
1/3 CUP SLICED GREEN ONIONS.
2 TEASPOONS LEMON JUICE.
1/2 TEASPOON KOSHER SALT ,
(MORE TO TASTE)

To make easy chicken salad, start by combining the diced cooked chicken, mayonnaise, celery, green onions, lemon juice and salt together in a large bowl. Stir the ingredients until everything is evenly mixed. Taste and adjust seasonings as desired. Serve this delicious chicken salad with crackers or bread for lunch or dinner. It's also great for making sandwiches or wraps. Enjoy!

For a variation, you can add in some of your favorite ingredients like chopped olives, diced apples, dried cranberries, shredded cheese or even grapes. Get creative and make this easy chicken salad unique to your own taste! This is also a great way to use up any leftover cooked chicken you have. If you're looking for a healthier version, try substituting Greek yogurt for the mayonnaise and adding lots of fresh herbs. Enjoy!

This easy chicken salad is a great dish to add to your menu rotation. It's quick, delicious and versatile. Plus, it's sure to be a hit with the whole family. Serve it with your favorite sides for an easy and tasty lunch or dinner! Enjoy!

Tofu Sandwich

Are you looking for vegetarian recipes for kids? Then look no further than this delicious tofu sandwich. It's a healthy and easy meal that your children will adore. Start by toasting some of their favorite bread, and spread with Thousand Island dressing. To make the sandwich extra special, add lettuce, tomatoes, avocado, cucumber and sprouts. This vegetarian recipe is sure to please everyone in the family! To prepare it, simply assemble all of the ingredients into the sandwich and serve. Your kids will love it! Enjoy!

The tofu sandwich is a great vegetarian alternative for kids and makes a healthy, easy meal that can be prepared quickly. A delicious combination of toasted bread, Thousand Island dressing, lettuce, tomatoes, avocado, cucumber and sprouts makes this vegetarian recipe both nutritious and tasty. It's an ideal way to get your kids to enjoy vegetarian meals - just assemble the ingredients into the sandwich and serve! Your children will love it and you can feel good knowing they are getting their daily dose of veggies. Kids need all the nutrition they can get - so why not try this vegetarian recipe today? Enjoy!

Chinese Pork Rice Fried

Here's a list of ingredients for traditional Chinese pork fried rice:

Cooked white rice (leftover rice is best)
Pork, diced
Scrambled egg
Green onions (scallions), chopped
Soy sauce
Oyster sauce
Hoisin sauce (optional)
Sesame oil (optional)
Vegetable oil or peanut oil, for frying

Instructions:

Heat a large wok or frying pan over high heat. Add oil and swirl to coat the pan.

Add the diced pork and stir-fry for 2-3 minutes, until browned and crispy.

Add the scrambled egg to the pan and stir to combine with the pork. Cook for another minute, until the egg is fully cooked.

Add the cooked rice to the pan and use a spatula to break up any clumps. Stir-fry for 2-3 minutes, until the rice is heated through and coated with the sauces.

Add the green onions and stir to combine.

Drizzle a small amount of soy sauce, oyster sauce, and hoisin sauce over the top of the fried rice, to taste. Stir well to distribute the sauces evenly.

Drizzle a small amount of sesame oil over the top, if desired. Stir to combine.

Serve the pork fried rice hot, garnished with additional chopped green onions, if desired. Enjoy!

Carbonara Spaghetti

Carbonara spaghetti is a delicious recipe for kids to learn how to cook. The ingredients you will need are 100g of pancetta, 50g of pecorino cheese, 50g of parmesan, 3 large eggs, 350g of spaghetti, 2 plump garlic cloves (peeled and left whole), 50g unsalted butter, sea salt, and freshly ground black pepper. To begin cooking this delicious dish, bring a large saucepan of salted water to the boil. Add the spaghetti and cook until al dente (around 8-10 minutes). Meanwhile, fry the pancetta in a dry non-stick frying pan over moderate heat for about 5 minutes until lightly golden. Once cooked, set aside and keep warm. In a small bowl, mix together the pecorino cheese and parmesan with the eggs until you have a creamy sauce. Season well with salt and pepper. When the spaghetti is cooked, drain it, reserving some of the cooking water. Add the spaghetti to the pan with the pancetta and garlic, and stir everything together. Add the butter, stirring until melted. Pour over the egg mixture and toss everything together well with a little of the reserved cooking water - this will help to make it nice and creamy. Serve immediately while still warm. Enjoy!

This delicious carbonara spaghetti dish is sure to be a hit with the whole family. With just a few ingredients and simple steps, your kids can learn to make this delicious dinner in no time! Serve it with a fresh salad on the side for a delicious meal that everyone will love. Enjoy!

Spinach And Feta Pie

INGREDIENTS
400 G (14 OZ) SPINACH LEAVES, FRESH OR FROZEN.
FRESH NUTMEG.
SEA SALT AND FRESHLY GROUND PEPPER.
200 G (7 OZ) FETA.
SQUEEZE OF LEMON JUICE.
3-4 LARGE SHEETS OF READY-ROLLED PUFF PASTRY (PREFERABLY MADE WITH BUTTER)
1 EGG BEATEN WITH A DASH OF MILK FOR THE EGG WASH.

Spinach and feta pie is a healthy, low-budget recipe that is easy and fast to make. This savory dish consists of 400 grams (14 oz) of fresh or frozen spinach leaves, fresh nutmeg, sea salt, freshly ground pepper, 200 grams (7 oz) of feta cheese and a squeeze of lemon juice. To top it off, you'll need 3-4 large sheets of ready-rolled puff pastry (preferably made with butter). Once the ingredients are prepared, simply assemble and brush your pie with an egg wash beaten with a dash of milk. Then bake for 25 minutes or until golden brown in a preheated oven. You can serve this healthy and delicious pie as an appetizer, side dish or even main course. Enjoy!

Lemon Mushroom Chicken

Ingredients:

4 chicken breasts (about 3/4 pound total)
1 1/2 tbsp unsalted butter, divided
8 oz cremini mushrooms, sliced
1/4 tsp salt
1/2 cup dry sherry
1/4 cup lemon juice
1/2 cup heavy cream
2 1/2 cups baby spinach

Instructions:

Season the chicken breasts with salt and pepper.

In a large pan, heat 1 tbsp of butter over medium heat. Add the chicken breasts and cook for about 4-5 minutes on each side, or until golden brown and fully cooked. Remove the chicken from the pan and set aside.

In the same pan, add the remaining butter and sliced mushrooms. Cook the mushrooms for about 4-5 minutes, or until they are tender and lightly browned.

Add the sherry to the pan and use a wooden spoon to scrape the bottom of the pan to release any browned bits. Cook the sherry for about 2 minutes, or until it has reduced by half.

Add the lemon juice and heavy cream to the pan and stir to combine. Cook the sauce for about 2-3 minutes, or until it has thickened slightly.

Return the chicken breasts to the pan and add the baby spinach. Stir to combine and cook for about 2 minutes, or until the spinach has wilted.

Serve the chicken with the lemon mushroom sauce on top. Enjoy!

Creamy Chicken Pasta

Ingredients
500 g | 1lb large chicken breasts (or skinless boneless thighs)
Salt and pepper, to season.
1/2 tbsp olive oil, to fry the chicken.
1 tbsp unsalted butter.
3 garlic cloves, minced.
500 ml | 2 cups double / heavy cream (or you can use single cream)
50 g | ½ cup freshly grated Parmesan cheese.
1 tsp salt.

For delicious recipes for kids, try this Creamy Chicken Pasta! It's easy to make and takes less than 30 minutes. Start by seasoning the chicken breasts with salt and pepper. Heat oil in a large skillet over medium-high heat, then add the chicken breast. Cook until it turns golden brown on both sides, about 4 minutes per side. Once cooked, remove the chicken and set aside. In the same pan, melt butter over medium heat and add minced garlic. Cook for 1 minute until fragrant. Pour in the cream and bring it to a simmer before adding Parmesan cheese and salt. Stir everything together until combined, then add the cooked chicken back in the pan. Reduce heat to low and simmer for 10 minutes, stirring occasionally. Serve over cooked pasta of your choice and enjoy! With this delicious recipe, you can easily delight even the pickiest of eaters. Bon appetite!

Focaccia Pizza

If you're looking for delicious pizza recipes, then look no further than focaccia pizza! This popular Italian dish is simple to prepare and full of delicious tastes. To get started, you'll need the following ingredients: 3 cups (15oz/422g) all-purpose flour, ½ teaspoon instant yeast, 2 teaspoons salt, 1 ⅓ cups (10 ½oz/282ml) water at room temperature, 2 tablespoons olive oil, ½ cup (4oz/115g) pizza sauce, 1 ½ cups (8oz/225g) mozzarella grated, and 10-12 pepperoni slices (optional).

To begin preparing this delicious dish, preheat your oven to 450°F. In a large bowl, mix together the flour, yeast, and salt. Once that's done, add in the water and olive oil and stir until a dough is formed. Knead it for 5 minutes on a lightly floured surface. Grease a 14-inch baking pan with olive oil before transferring your dough to it. Press the dough into the pan using your fingertips to form an even layer. Brush with additional oil if needed, then bake at 450°F for 12 minutes.

Once the crust has cooked through, remove from oven and spread pizza sauce over top followed by mozzarella and pepperoni (if desired). Bake again for 10-15 minutes or until cheese is melted and bubbling. Let cool slightly before cutting into slices and serving. Enjoy your delicious focaccia pizza!

You can also customize this delicious dish by adding any additional toppings of your choice! From mushrooms to bell peppers, the possibilities are endless. Give it a try and let us know how delicious your focaccia pizza turned out! Bon Appétit!

Crispy Potato Tacos

INGREDIENTS

2 LARGE RUSSET POTATOES.
¾ CUP SOUR CREAM.
2 CLOVES GARLIC, MINCED.
½ TEASPOON CUMIN.
SALT, TO TASTE.
½ TEASPOON OREGANO.
8 CORN TORTILLAS.
OIL, FOR FRYING.

Crispy potato tacos are a healthy vegetarian recipe for kids that is easy to prepare. Start by preheating your oven to 400°F and scrubbing the potatoes clean. Cut them into thin slices, about ¼-inch thick, and place onto a baking sheet lined with parchment paper. Drizzle with oil and sprinkle with salt, then bake for 25 minutes or until golden brown.

While the potatoes are baking, make the sour cream garlic sauce by combining the sour cream, minced garlic, cumin, oregano and salt in a bowl. Mix ingredients until everything is well combined.

Once the potatoes have finished baking, heat up some oil in a large skillet over high heat. Place four of the tortillas in the skillet and cook for 30-45 seconds per side until lightly browned. Place them on a plate lined with paper towels to absorb any excess oil.

To assemble tacos, place two potato slices inside each tortilla, then top with some of the sour cream garlic sauce and fold in half. Repeat this process with the remaining four tortillas and serve immediately. Enjoy!

These vegetarian crispy potato tacos are sure to be a hit amongst kids and adults alike! So next time you're looking for an easy, healthy vegetarian recipe for kids, try making these delicious tacos. They'll definitely make dinner time much more fun!

Chicken And Creamy Bacon Penne

Ingredients

1 tbsp olive oil.
2 boneless skinless chicken breasts.
100g smoked lardon (chopped bacon)
4 tbsp dry white wine.
100g frozen petits pois.
5 tbsp double cream.
8220g packet cooked penne.!

Chicken with creamy bacon penne is a delicious recipe for kids that's easy to cook. Begin by heating the olive oil in a large non-stick pan and adding the chicken breasts. Cook these until golden brown, then add the chopped lardon (bacon) and fry until crisp. Next, pour in the white wine, stirring continuously to prevent sticking. Once the wine has reduced by half, add in small handfuls of frozen petits pois and stir until cooked through.

Finally, reduce to a low heat and add in the double cream and cooked penne. Stir continuously for 4-5 minutes until all ingredients are combined and creamy sauce is formed. Serve hot for delicious family meal. Enjoy!

Avocado Fusilli Pasta

Ingredients

350g fusilli.
2 cloves garlic, peeled.
200g baby spinach.
2 small ripe avocados, halved and stoned.
extra-virgin olive oil, for drizzling.
30g roasted cashews, chopped.
30g roasted almonds, chopped.
a small bunch coriander, chopped.

For healthy and delicious pasta, you can't go wrong with this avocado fusilli recipe! Start by bringing a large pot of salted water to the boil. Add the fusilli and cook until al dente. Meanwhile, in a large pan over medium heat, add some olive oil and garlic cloves. Saute for 5 minutes until fragrant. Add the baby spinach and cook for a few minutes until wilted. When the pasta is cooked, drain it and add to the pan with the spinach mixture. Finally, top with halved avocados, roasted cashews and almonds and chopped coriander. Drizzle with some extra-virgin olive oil for a healthy finish. Serve and enjoy! This healthy pasta dish is sure to become a favorite in your house. With its creamy avocado, crunchy nuts, and delicious flavors from the garlic, spinach and coriander, it's an easy healthy meal that everyone can enjoy. Try this avocado fusilli recipe today!

Lemon Butter Fish

Ingredients lemon butterfish

1 lb white fish, about four 4-oz fillets- I used halibut.
1 1/2 tbsp olive oil.
1 tsp paprika.
1 tsp garlic powder.
1/2 tsp salt.
1/2 tsp black pepper.
Lemon Butter Sauce.
1/4 cup butter.

Instructions:

Preheat your oven to 400°F (200°C). Line a large baking sheet with parchment paper or lightly grease with cooking spray.

In a small bowl, mix together the olive oil, paprika, garlic powder, salt, and pepper.

Place the fish fillets on the prepared baking sheet. Brush both sides of the fish with the olive oil mixture.

Bake for 10-12 minutes, or until the fish is opaque and flakes easily with a fork.

While the fish is baking, make the lemon butter sauce. In a small saucepan, melt the butter over medium heat. Add freshly squeezed lemon juice, minced garlic, and dried herbs (such as thyme or basil) to taste. Stir to combine and cook for 1-2 minutes until the sauce is heated through.

Remove the baked fish from the oven and transfer to a serving platter. Spoon the lemon butter sauce over the top of each fish fillet.

Serve the lemon butter fish hot with your favorite side dishes, such as roasted vegetables or a fresh salad.

Enjoy your delicious and flavorful lemon butter fish!

Roasted Black Bean Burger

Ingredients

1½ red onions.
200 g mixed mushrooms.
100 g rye bread.
ground coriander.
1 x 400 g tin of black beans.
40 g mature Cheddar cheese.
4 soft rolls.
100 g ripe cherry tomatoes.

Instructions

Preheat the oven to 200°C (180°C fan) / 400°F / Gas Mark 6. Line a baking sheet with parchment paper.

Chop the red onions and mushrooms into small pieces and roast them on the prepared baking sheet for 10-15 minutes or until they are soft and lightly browned.

Cut the rye bread into small cubes and place in a large bowl.

Drain and rinse the black beans and add them to the bowl with the bread cubes.

Grate the Cheddar cheese and add it to the bowl with the bread and beans.

Add the roasted onions and mushrooms to the bowl, along with 2 teaspoons of ground coriander.

Mash the mixture together using a fork or potato masher, until it forms a sticky, cohesive mixture.

Divide the mixture into 4 portions and form each portion into a patty.

Place the patties on the prepared baking sheet and bake in the preheated oven for 15-20 minutes, or until they are firm and crispy.

While the burgers are baking, slice the soft rolls and halve the cherry tomatoes.

Once the burgers are cooked, assemble the sandwiches by placing a patty in each roll and topping with cherry tomato slices. Serve immediately. Enjoy!

Cheesy Broccoli Pasta

Ingredients
½ cup butter.
1 onion, chopped. Fresh Onions.
1 (16 ounce) package frozen chopped broccoli.
4 (14.5 ounce) cans chicken broth.
1 (1 pound) loaf processed cheese food, cubed.
2 cups milk.
1 tablespoon garlic powder.
⅔ cup cornstarch.

This delicious cheesy broccoli pasta is a sure hit for kids and adults alike! With just a few simple steps, anyone can make this delicious dish in no time.

First, melt the butter in a large pot over medium heat. Add the chopped onion and cook until softened, about 5 minutes. Next, add the frozen chopped broccoli and chicken broth and bring to a boil. Reduce the heat, cover, and simmer for 15 minutes.

Once done, add the cubed cheese food, milk, garlic powder and cornstarch to the pot. Give it all a good stir then cover and cook for about 10 more minutes or until the sauce has thickened. Serve hot with your favorite sides!

This cheesy broccoli pasta is delicious and easy to make, making it an ideal recipe for kids. If you're looking for a delicious and nutritious dish that your whole family can enjoy, this is the perfect choice! So what are you waiting for? Try out this delicious cheesy broccoli pasta today!

Enjoy

I want to take a moment to express my heartfelt gratitude for your recent purchase of my recipe book. As a passionate food lover, nothing makes me happier than sharing my favorite recipes with others. Your decision to invest in my book not only supports my dream, but also shows your commitment to expanding your culinary horizons.

I sincerely hope that the recipes in the book will inspire you to try new things and add some excitement to your meals.

Thank you again for your support and for being a part of this journey with me. I hope my book will bring you many happy and delicious moments in the kitchen.

www.ingramcontent.com/pod-product-compliance
Lightning Source LLC
Chambersburg PA
CBHW041151110526
44590CB00027B/4189